Life of a Busy Bee

Sue Messruther

Copyright © 2018 Sue Messruther

First Printing, 2018

Dedication

To the busiest Queen Bee I know... My daughter Rosheen, a brilliant leader of the team... Queen Bees.

Contents

January

S	M	T	W	T	F	S
		1	2	3	4	5
6	7	8	9	10	11	12
13	14	15	16	17	18	19
20	21	22	23	24	25	26
27	28	29	30	31		

1	
2	
3	
4	

5	
6	
7	
8	

9	
10	
11	
12	

13	
14	
15	
16	

17	
18	
19	
20	

21	
22	
23	
24	

25	
26	
27	
28	

29

30

31

February

S	M	T	W	T	F	S
					1	2
3	4	5	6	7	8	9
10	11	12	13	14	15	16
17	18	19	20	21	22	23
24	25	26	27	28		

1	
2	
3	
4	

5	
6	
7	
8	

9	
10	
11	
12	

13

14

15

16

17	
18	
19	
20	

21	
22	
23	
24	

25	
26	
27	
28	

March

<table>
<tr><td>S</td><td>M</td><td>T</td><td>W</td><td>T</td><td>F</td><td>S</td></tr>
<tr><td></td><td></td><td></td><td></td><td></td><td>1</td><td>2</td></tr>
<tr><td>3</td><td>4</td><td>5</td><td>6</td><td>7</td><td>8</td><td>9</td></tr>
<tr><td>10</td><td>11</td><td>12</td><td>13</td><td>14</td><td>15</td><td>16</td></tr>
<tr><td>17</td><td>18</td><td>19</td><td>20</td><td>21</td><td>22</td><td>23</td></tr>
<tr><td>24</td><td>25</td><td>26</td><td>27</td><td>28</td><td>29</td><td>30</td></tr>
<tr><td>31</td><td></td><td></td><td></td><td></td><td></td><td></td></tr>
</table>

1	
2	
3	
4	

5	
6	
7	
8	

9

10

11

12

13

14

15

16

17	
18	
19	
20	

21	
22	
23	
24	

25	
26	
27	
28	

29	
30	
31	

April

S	M	T	W	T	F	S
	1	2	3	4	5	6
7	8	9	10	11	12	13
14	15	16	17	18	19	20
21	22	23	24	25	26	27
28	29	30				

1	
2	
3	
4	

5	
6	
7	
8	

9	
10	
11	
12	

13	
14	
15	
16	

17	
18	
19	
20	

21	
22	
23	
24	

25	
26	
27	
28	

29

30

May

S	M	T	W	T	F	S
			1	2	3	4
5	6	7	8	9	10	11
12	13	14	15	16	17	18
19	20	21	22	23	24	25
26	27	28	29	30	31	

1	
2	
3	
4	

5	
6	
7	
8	

9	
10	
11	
12	

13	
14	
15	
16	

17

18

19

20

21	
22	
23	
24	

25

26

27

28

29

30

31

June

<pre>
S   M   T   W   T   F   S
                        1
2   3   4   5   6   7   8
9 10 11 12 13 14 15
16 17 18 19 20 21 22
23 24 25 26 27 28 29
30
</pre>

1	
2	
3	
4	

5	
6	
7	
8	

9	
10	
11	
12	

13

14

15

16

17

18

19

20

21	
22	
23	
24	

25	
26	
27	
28	

29

30

July

S	M	T	W	T	F	S
	1	2	3	4	5	6
7	8	9	10	11	12	13
14	15	16	17	18	19	20
21	22	23	24	25	26	27
28	29	30	31			

1	
2	
3	
4	

5	
6	
7	
8	

9

10

11

12

13	
14	
15	
16	

17	
18	
19	
20	

21	
22	
23	
24	

25	
26	
27	
28	

29

30

31

August

S	M	T	W	T	F	S
				1	2	3
4	5	6	7	8	9	10
11	12	13	14	15	16	17
18	19	20	21	22	23	24
25	26	27	28	29	30	31

1

2

3

4

5	
6	
7	
8	

9	
10	
11	
12	

13

14

15

16

17

18

19

20

21	
22	
23	
24	

25	
26	
27	
28	

29	
30	
31	

September

S	M	T	W	T	F	S
1	2	3	4	5	6	7
8	9	10	11	12	13	14
15	16	17	18	19	20	21
22	23	24	25	26	27	28
29	30					

1	
2	
3	
4	

5	
6	
7	
8	

9	
10	
11	
12	

13	
14	
15	
16	

17	
18	
19	
20	

21

22

23

24

25	
26	
27	
28	

29

30

October

S	M	T	W	T	F	S
		1	2	3	4	5
6	7	8	9	10	11	12
13	14	15	16	17	18	19
20	21	22	23	24	25	26
27	28	29	30	31		

1

2

3

4

5	
6	
7	
8	

9

10

11

12

13

14

15

16

17

18

19

20

21	
22	
23	
24	

25	
26	
27	
28	

29

30

31

November

S	M	T	W	T	F	S
					1	2
3	4	5	6	7	8	9
10	11	12	13	14	15	16
17	18	19	20	21	22	23
24	25	26	27	28	29	30

1	
2	
3	
4	

5	
6	
7	
8	

9

10

11

12

13

14

15

16

17

18

19

20

21	
22	
23	
24	

25

26

27

28

29	
30	

December

S	M	T	W	T	F	S
1	2	3	4	5	6	7
8	9	10	11	12	13	14
15	16	17	18	19	20	21
22	23	24	25	26	27	28
29	30	31				

1	
2	
3	
4	

<table>
<tr><td>5</td><td></td></tr>
<tr><td>6</td><td></td></tr>
<tr><td>7</td><td></td></tr>
<tr><td>8</td><td></td></tr>
</table>

9

10

11

12

13	
14	
15	
16	

17	
18	
19	
20	

21	
22	
23	
24	

25	
26	
27	
28	

29

30

31

About The

Author

Born in Adelaide, South Australia, Sue Messruther has written many well-reviewed books, a good mix for adults and children as Sue is a mother of 6 children and currently 6 grandchildren. She loves her allotment and spends many hours weeding, watering and planning next year's crops, even here her humour shines through as her allotment has street signs!

She has created many adult colouring books, journals and organisers these just continue to grow as inspiration guides her onto the next book.

Sue's children's books are a true delight as she composes all of the images around the stories she creates. Her bestselling children's volume sets include the Just For Kids series, Alien Caper Encounters series and the Dogs, Cats & All Other Animals and let's not forget Messruther's stand-alone titles which include Santa's Christmas: The Year the Sleigh Broke Down, Christmas Home Made Cookie Gifts, and 30 Best Breads from Around the World.

Sue enjoys creating & colouring in her Adult Colouring Books & Journals, some of these have space to add extra doodles, others that are simple and then many images that are challenging! So she does create and use her own books, in fact many of the journals were created because she had a need for them and her colouring books she needed these for the dementia patients she looks after in her full time job.

Messruther has also contributed writings to the books Thorns to be Thankful For and Skill Share both of which became best sellers in the first week of publication.

There are always more books in the creation cycle for example a new children's series currently in various stages is the Play Time Books, which forthcoming from the author, of which Come Find Me Under The Sea is the first to arrive in this series followed by Back In Time With Dinosaurs and then It's A Dog's Life. Titles after this are yet to be determined!

Messruther has lived in Cairns, Queensland, Australia and now currently resides in Scarborough, North Yorkshire, England, with her family and Oscar, an Old English Sheep puppy of gigantic proportions, (Digby is a constant thought and fear, and will Oscar grow that big!) Thankfully, his growth has slowed down now so Digby II is safe from reality!

As with everyone, her life and inspirations grow on a daily basis so the future is looking very creative indeed to follow up with new titles you can contact Sue Messruther on her facebook page https://www.facebook.com/suemessruther.author/ she would love to hear from you and you can follow her progress.

Other Titles

My Life

Bit By Bit

Step By Step

One Step at a Time

One Day at a Time

Month by Month

Day by Day

Through The Year

Every Day Is New

I Made It!

Another Year

Monthly Journals

Dear Me

Good Gracious

Gee Whiz

Goodness Me

Gracious Me

What a Day

Today I

It All Began When

Here and Now

I Accomplished

I Want

Look At Me

Moment Journals

Just Thinking

I Am Me

All that I am

Within Me

Believing In Me

Quietly I Am

About Me

Organisers

My Organiser - That's Life

My Organiser - I Rule

My Organiser - For The Weekends

My Organiser - Fantasy

My Organiser - Flower power

My Organiser - Puppy love

My Organiser - Perrrrfect Days

2019 Diaries

Life of a Busy Bee

A Whimsical Year

Family Affair

Beast Of Me